Living the Magic

A Walk on the Lighter Side

᭬᭬

Michael Delaware

If, And or But
Publishing Company

Published by
'If, And or But' Publishing Company
P.O. Box 2559
Battle Creek, Michigan 49016 USA
www.ifandorbutpublishing.com

ISBN-13: 978-0615979182
ISBN-10: 0615979181

Cover photos are licensed images obtained through BigStockPhotos.com.

In Memory of
Dwight Matheny

Table of Contents:

Introduction

I wrote this book to share some of the lessons I have learned in my own life that have raised my awareness to the magic in living. I call it *'living the magic'* and it is about having a compassion for others in life, and tapping into that excitement of living. The *joy of laughter*, the *warmth of goodwill* and the sensation of *that spiritual lift* are some of the things you will discover within this book.

The chapters are drawn from my life experiences, and are a collection of essays on my observations and conclusions. I have long sought to live a more spiritual life in greater proportion to that of materialism. As with many people, it is never easy.

Within these pages I hope I can inspire you into action with forwarding a message of goodwill, kindness and compassion to anyone you interact with including complete strangers. In doing so, perhaps we can all get to know each other a little better and soon there will be no strangers and only a world of approachable friends.

Chapter One:

When We Were Babies...

Have you ever looked at a happy baby? I had an experience in a grocery store with my wife, and she was looking at some items on a shelf. I was standing with the shopping cart waiting for her to make her selection adrift in my own thoughts. Across the aisle from me was a mother with her baby sitting in a safety seat on her cart.

The baby's mother was engaged, much like my wife, in looking at items on another shelf. The little baby and I made eye contact. She was a beautiful little girl, maybe a year old and she was just looking. When she locked eyes on me, she just looked at me peacefully, with an unblinking countenance. She then smiled and started to laugh.

Do you know what happened then? I found myself smiling too. In fact I felt like laughing and laughed aloud. Soon the baby girl and I were just looking at each other and laughing.

4

Isn't it amazing how babies can teach us something so simple about experiencing joy in life? There was nothing special to laugh at, or about. She just looked at me, and I at her, and she decided to release some laughter. She liked me, or perhaps she still had that keen sense to know she could and should release some joyous laughter in me. Perhaps she knew I was lost in thought, and needed to come back to the present and laugh.

One could almost go so far as to suggest that many children up to a certain age possess a particular talent that somehow gets lost as they grow up. It is a power to release joy in others, and also to see into people and bring something good out in them.

It is a skill that many adults have forgotten, though we all had this skill at one time in our childhood. That ability to simply look at someone, touch them with your soul with just a glimmer in your eyes, a smile on your face or a good sincere laugh. Babies and little children possess this ability.

Some children do not have this ability long, or so it seems, and one could assume this gift is as manifest as to the proportion of love in their life. If the parents or family do not openly love the child, then perhaps the child can feel the absence of such and so this ability goes away. Or perhaps it is directed elsewhere, rather than outward at strangers in a grocery store.

Whatever the case may be, it is a very precise magic, one could say. A special gift involving the ability to cross space with just a mere look and a smile, followed by a joyous giggle, to lift the spirits of another. It is a lost magic to many in the world of grown-ups, but one we should all try to emulate and rediscover within the dark corners of our soul.

Chapter Two:

The Only Good Medicine

Have you ever had one of those grand old belly laughs with a friend about something? It does not matter what the subject was, or who it was with, it is just the laugh. If you think about it for a moment, that laugh you had really made you feel good didn't it?

Sure, if you laughed long and hard until you cried, you might have felt a slight bit fatigued when you stopped. However, I would venture to guess that you also felt a sense of refreshment of the soul following that moment. It was so refreshing that you could probably close your eyes right now, and if you revisit that moment in time and in the present, you might feel a residue of joy in your heart from recalling that experience.

That is the precise and exact essence of the human experience. Laughter is the only good medicine. It spans time and location, and crosses all divisions of ethnicity, language and culture. It touches all age groups, and all genders.

Laughter heals the soul. It can put out the fires of hostility, and bridge the boundaries of understanding. It can heal the broken-hearted, and lift the weary soul.

I once worked for a call center answering calls on an addiction hotline. One evening a woman who had been drinking heavily called in stating that she wanted my help in finding a rehabilitation center near where her sister lived in Arizona.

I looked up center locations for her and gave her the numbers to call. She wrote them down, and had to ask me to repeat them over and over again because she was intoxicated. She began to tell me her story, and it was a sad one. Her son had committed suicide a year prior and her husband who was so heartbroken about the incident had taken his own life just eight months later.

She was devastated, and had turned to drinking to numb the pain. I talked to her and just listened for almost an hour. She told me the story again and again. Eventually after just being calm and friendly with her, and reminding her over and over again to call the rehab centers I had given her, she began to lighten up and stopped crying.

Towards the end of the phone call she was laughing, and I could sense that she felt a release of tension and unspoken feelings just by having taken time to reach out and speak with me, a complete stranger to her. The laughter eased her pain, and lifted her spirits. It was good medicine. It was the medicine she needed.

There is another story I would like to share here that has great relevance to this chapter. It is something that occurred to me right out in front of my home one July evening.

It was a mildly warm night and my wife had the front windows opened because it was so nice outside. I was passing by my front dining room, when I heard shouting outside coming from the neighbor's house.

I went out on the front porch, and saw a young man in a heated argument with a woman and a young girl out on the front lawn next to mine. I stood there on my front porch and merely observed the tirade.

At one point the young man in a fit of anger turned to me and said *"What are you looking at? Go back in your house!"* I merely stood there and looked at him.

He came storming over to my lawn and approached my porch in anger and said again *"What are you looking at?"* The girl on the lawn was begging him not to come over.

I said to him as he approached very sincerely and kindly *"I am looking at a man with tremendous potential, who looks like he could use some help."* He stopped in his tracks and looked at me. I suppose he was expecting some typical antagonistic rebuttal so he could provoke a fight.

I continued to look at him, and it was obvious he was in a quandary. His morals would not permit him to strike a woman, or a child, so he was looking for the next likely target who happened to be the man looking at him from his porch. When he approached me, I was not hostile, but civil and kind. I did not engage him with the same negative vibrations that were racing through him, but merely smiled and looked at him.

I spoke to him again in a voice of kindness *"I am interested in helping you, because I think you could use it"* following up with a friendly laugh.
He looked at me and asked *"So you weren't trying to help them?"* pointing to the obviously shaken woman and girl on the lawn.

I said to him and laughed *"You came on my lawn, my friend, so I am interested in helping you. Why don't you come over and tell me what's happening?"*

So he looked down and then back at me, and you could see his anger subside. All I had shown to him was kindness and friendship.

He came over and began to tell me all about his problems with his fiancé and their relationship. I listened and acknowledged what he told me, and just simply became a voice of reason for him. He had no one in his life that would listen or that he felt he could talk to.

So we sat on my porch for over an hour talking about his relationship, his job, his plans and anything he wanted to talk about. It was a delightful experience in the end, and I made a good friend, and so did he.

At one point I had him genuinely laughing about his life, his relationship and the troubles he had created. In the end I suggested that he give the girl some flowers and make peace, and be brave enough to swallow his pride and apologize.

The outcome was that I saved a young woman and child from a particularly upsetting evening and a young man from getting himself arrested on a domestic violence charge or some other such problem from the quarrel had it escalated further.

I merely used laughter and kindness to help defuse his anger, and in a matter of minutes he became civil and opened up. The real problem was that he needed someone to talk to who would listen. Laughter helped with the medicine, and it was genuine laughter, not ridicule that eased his burden.

There were no more fights between his girlfriend and himself that summer, and we saw each other off and on as neighbors. He later moved away, and I wished him well as he departed.

A great deal could be said about just taking time to talk to someone, listen to their stories and let them know you have heard them. It can unburden their soul and lighten their hearts. If they begin to laugh, then it is all the better. The laughter is the final medicine where the heart mends the fractures in the soul, and like a sand castle as evening tide moves in and settles all the ripples again into a smooth, even surface.

Laughter heals the soul in more ways than can be told. The more one laughs, the better one feels overall, and a happier outlook they will have on life. The only good medicine in life is *laughter.*

Chapter Three:

A Diet of Daily Laughter

Far too often one can slide into a mental state where life is too serious. Seriousness after a time removes all the smiles from ones surroundings. If one can raise one's own head for a moment above this seriousness, and consider something *unserious* for a moment, one just might *laugh*.

Laughter has long been regarded as powerful spiritual healing power. Much has been written about this throughout history and literature. An ancient biblical proverb once claimed *"A merry heart doeth good like medicine"* asserting the power of laughter for its healing properties.

Medical studies have shown that laughter can also strengthen the immune system, boost your energy and reduce physical pain. There is no greater stress reliever than a good rolling laugh. Laughter is a simple and easy way to reduce stress, pain and conflict in the environment as well.

Soldiers who serve together in war often share stories of laughter and fun with their brothers-in-arms more readily than their experiences on the battlefield. Laughter is more easily remembered because it brings joy.

In ancient times the court jester was brought in to ease tensions and relieve melancholy and bring merriment to royalty. Native American tribes like the Hopi and Cree had clown characters in their traditional ceremonies whose job was to provoke laughter and bring about lightheartedness.

Laughter is infectious. The sound of roaring in laughter is far more contagious than any symptom of influenza. When one has a good hearty shared laugh with another, it binds us together in a way that did not exist before. To be able to laugh uncontrollably in uproarious laughter with a colleague, family member or friend may increase general overall happiness. When one laughs together with family it fosters open communication, understanding and harmony. There is no more unmistakably powerful undercurrent to bringing people together than a genuine good laugh with those one loves.

The power of mirth can extend to any group and bring about a healthy relationship and serve as a binding agent that's hard to separate. There is no better way to bring people together than to include some good hearty laughter and merriment in the course of a day. If one can sincerely laugh, he or she can get others to laugh as well, because it is infectious.

If you think for a moment about the last really good laugh you had, how did you feel? It probably made you feel better than you feel right now, didn't it? Laughter is safer and far more effective to a person's well being than any pill produced by Big Pharma. There is nothing quite like a jiggling good ol' belly laugh with your eyes watering to really make your day feel lighter.

So if you want a diet of really good medicine, remember to laugh and laugh often. Be of good cheer and encourage others to laugh as well.

18

Laughter can bring harmony, and it might just be the best secret ever.

Chapter Four:

The Circle of Vitality

In our global culture of instant communication, we can talk to someone on the other side of the world right from our desktop computer. We can make friends or create enemies with our fingertips. It is easy to understand that despite physical distances, we all have a connection at a spiritual level, whether one wants to believe it or not.

We see more changes economically, where one country in Europe can have a disaster with the crash of an industry, and the impact of is felt in the stock markets of New York and London. The world is connected on many levels, and our civilization has always been this way to a greater or lesser degree.

In the time of Marco Polo, the trade routes were beginning to open, and the Orient once again, after many centuries, was connected once more with European civilization. Following the exploration of the Vikings and Christopher Columbus, the Americas became connected or re-discovered, (depending on how you look at history) and thus, connecting the world even further in the centuries that followed.

In our present time, the last twenty years or so have seen the world connected by the internet. When the internet began, commerce moved slowly due to trepidation and uncertainty. That was the early 1990's. Twenty years later, e-Commerce in 2012 surpassed 14 Billion dollars in the U.S. alone as estimated by the Census Bureau in the Department of Commerce.

Just as commerce and trade has expanded, so have international relations. Classrooms of school children interact daily with children from all over the world through the miracle of modern technology. The world, as vast as it is, is a much closer and closely connected place online.

The word **vitality** means: *'The state of being strong and active; energy'*. It is also has another definition which reads: *'The power of giving continuance of life, present in all living things'.*

It is this second definition that I refer to here. It is the interconnection that we all share that brings about our continuance in life as a global civilization. When we act with compassion and kindness to others and treat each other with courtesy and respect, despite differences in opinion or doctrine of belief, we may be extending the life continuance with positive energy. When we do otherwise, we may be extinguishing life with negative energy.

It is in this positive energy that we can keep alive the circle of vitality. Man has been progressing forward with technological advancements, but he has been lagging at a slower pace with his spiritual awareness. He loses sight of the interconnected circle he is part of, and instead disrupts that harmony with perceived ideological and cultural differences.

Part of that living magic of life is to know that one can laugh, embrace and share ideas with anyone despite their location or background or belief structure. It is a circle you are part of, where no one is insignificant and each and everyone is responsible for doing their part to create that universal harmony.

Chapter Five:

The Spiritual Lift

When I was twelve years old, I went with my Boy Scout troop to the Grand Canyon for a hiking trip. We drove all night, and arrived in the early hours of the morning on the rim of the canyon near the trail head. The journey was in the dark, and as I have never been able to sleep soundly in a moving car, I was wide awake most of the trip there.

When we reached the parking or staging area near the trailhead, we all slept for a few hours before dawn. Sometime around 5am one of the men who were helping with the trip set up a stove and cooked up a massive batch of pancakes. I woke up to the smell of sausages on a skittle, surrounded by an orange glow of the sun creeping over the horizon.

Within an hour the entire troop was fed, and the sun was still low on the horizon, but the day was getting brighter. I remember feeling very nervous, as from where we were parked I could not see a trail head. I had been afraid there was going to be a steep decent down, or some sort of dangerous trip ahead. I ate very little of the breakfast offered.

I can remember standing on the rim of the Canyon looking out over its great expanse which seemed to go on forever, and the bright colors and shadows of orange, gold and brown as if the sun was painting the scene like a morning portrait for me alone.

We strapped on our backpacks, and were organized into a marching line and proceeded to walk towards the opposite end of the parking lot we had temporarily camped at. It was cool and I was wearing a light jacket, although I had been told that as the day progressed I would be shedding that soon enough.

To my relief we approached a trailhead that was an easy decline traveling along the sandstone wall, descending into the Canyon. We hiked farther down the trail at that time of the morning it was still dark despite the sun beginning to rise, as we were within the shadow of the Canyon wall.

As we progressed down the trail, it zigzagged along the canyon wall, every turn we took bringing our group that much closer to the bottom. I recall when the first section of our group arrived at the base of the Canyon; we took a break and waited for the others who had fallen behind.

I can remember feeling proud of myself at that moment for the speed in which we had made the descent covering such a great distance down the trail. It was reported that we had already traveled two miles, however, this being one of my first hikes, this success soon turned out to be an illusion. It is one thing to descend two miles down a declining trail in the cool morning temperatures, and quite another to travel the same distance on a flat gravel and sand trail exposed to the full sun. Yes, quite a difference indeed.

After a head count was taken, we shed our jackets, again hoisted our packs upon our backs and continued on down the trail. Little did I know this would be the last time we would all see each other as an entire group until we reached our final destination.

The sun was much higher in the sky at this point, and as the trail left the shadow of the canyon wall, we were without the benefit of shade. As I mentioned before, the trail became loose gravel that caused one's foot to slip a few inches with every step. Eventually the trail surface became a mixture of red sand and stone after few more miles, thus adding the adversity of the occasional twist to the ankle. One soon learned to pay attention to foot placement, looking downward frequently as we hiked.

All in all we hiked the entirety of the day. The group spreading out, until it reached a point where the stragglers (my eventual group) had not seen anyone in our troop for many hours. Ultimately, as mentioned we all rendezvoused at the final campground at the end of a long and tiresome day.

I will not at this time go into the nitty-gritty details of the entirety of that hike, but only will say it was a long, hard and tiresome experience for me. I learned a great deal about perseverance on that first hike in the Grand Canyon. I learned that one can truly march on, despite all mental rebuttals in one's head that they cannot. It was perhaps my first great challenge in my early youth, and when I look back on it after all these years it was a wonderful experience.

When we finally arrived at the camp, I was able to shed my backpack and walk freely around for an hour without the concern of having to tote its burden farther down the trail, at least not for the rest of that day.

That spiritual lift one feels after carrying a heavy load for so long a period of time is quite remarkable. There is a physical feeling of relief to be certain, but there is also an unburdening that happens simultaneously with the soul. It is the end of an arduous journey, and one can relax for a time and rejoice.

Our trip schedule unfortunately was poorly planned. Instead of spending a full day in the campground and giving everyone an extra day of relaxation, we were to return back up the same trail we had hiked the very next day. It was a mere two day hiking trip.

The return trip was even more challenging. Not only were we tired from the prior day's exhaustion, but after having slept on hard ground or on or in an uncomfortable sleeping bag, it was exceptionally brutal to begin the march. Further, one still had those final two miles to look forward to now at the end of the hike, which consisted up *ascending the trail* this time up the Canyon wall.

To top it all off, squirrels had breached my backpack while I slept and consumed all of my trail mix, and a good portion of my breakfast food. My father was fortunately on the hike with me, and his pack was unmolested. Between his food and what remained of my own, along with some charity from our fellow hikers, we managed a breakfast.

Once again the day was long and the sun was hot. When hiking in the Grand Canyon the trail tends to always be disappearing around the next bend in the rock walls. It is kind of defeating, in a way. One pushes with all their energy to reach that bend in the trail hoping to see beyond and lay one's eyes on the journey, only to see another leg in the trail and yet another bend.

Call it the disappearing trail of life or the deceiving illusion of hope if you will. I remember at times feeling that I should just collapse and spend the rest of my days on that trail and it would all be fine as long as I did not have to take another step.

I am sure my backpack was tremendously overweight for my size, as these were the old military-style canvas single frame packs. Ultra light packs would not be invented for another decade or more. Still, I trudged along the trail and set my goals for every bend to see beyond the next canyon stone outcropping.
Eventually after another day-long toil and progressive stumbling, we arrived at the base of the winding trail of switchbacks.

At first glance upward, it looks pretty benign. It
is only when one is ten or more minutes up the
trail that the realization hits that you have only
progressed a few hundred yards at best. You
soon realize that if you thought the day up until
then had been tough, *hell was before you.*

The Canyon trail has that unnerving way of
having the trail disappear upward out of sight,
and when you reach that rise in the trail, there is
another one revealed before you doing the same.
Over and over, the trail deceives and annoys you
hour after hour. The backpack on my back
seemed to grow heavier with every step upward,
and the day seemed like it would never end.

However the trail did finally end after another
three hours of slow upward hiking. Once again I
dropped my backpack off near the cars, and felt
again that spiritual uplift of freedom starting
with the lightness of the body.

I realized soon enough that spiritually I had been
through a journey as much as my body had. I was
physically exhausted, but revitalized. There was

no describing the transcendent feeling of having been through such a wearisome expedition into the Grand Canyon.

It was a spiritual lift that I would remember for years to come. Many times I find myself reliving that experience on some sort of ethereal plane within my heart and soul. A ripple of energy sometimes runs through me when I recall that time, and that journey.

I realized that the uplifting exultation or euphoria from the completion that I felt after our weekend trek was something not everyone experiences. As hard as it is to describe, it is even harder to convince others that they too must take such a journey to show them what it means to feel that level of exuberance about accomplishing something. If they can do that, then perhaps there would be less materialism in the world and more spiritualism.

Call it a spiritual lift, a renewal or a simple raised awareness. This hike for me at that age, and under those conditions opened doors for me I never would have opened had I not persevered and completed that trail. In the end, there was serenity to that moment that is to this day difficult to convey to others who have never taken such a journey.

It was a spiritual lift that I believe all should acquaint themselves with.

Chapter Six:

Goodwill is Infectious

Goodwill could best be defined as *'having a friendly, helpful or cooperative feeling towards another or others.'* Goodwill is, in essence, doing good things for others. It quite often takes the role of making sure that positive feelings are forwarded to others. Goodwill, once one unselfishly engages in it for a time to help others, is infectious. It is something that can become habit forming and can spread to others.

Practicing goodwill requires no other quality that having a heart and caring for others. It is taking time to reach out to others and help them with or without their stepping forward and asking for that help.

Goodwill can become infectious when it is sincere, and even more, when the recipients are in genuine need. When these two elements are in play, the person providing goodwill are compelled to do more, and the recipient can become inspired to reciprocate with goodwill towards others.

In the late 1990's I was living in the Atlanta area, with my brother Robert who came up with the inspiring idea to do some goodwill one holiday season. He had heard on a news show on television that the local Post Office receives hundreds of letters to Santa every season, and they were coordinating with a local charity to help the children with a legitimate need.

My brother got inspired by this and asked to be sent five of the Santa letters, intending to fulfill them. He had very little prediction as to what to expect. What he received were very long lists, much longer than he had imagined. Not backing down from the challenge, he recruited me and other family members to help him pull together items on the list. Soon the project became a group activity.

We called friends and asked for donated toys and games, etc. What we could not get donated; we went to the store and purchased. We packaged all the gifts into their respective groupings and began making plans to deliver them. The instructions from the charity organization were to place the items in the hands of a taxi driver and have them delivered anonymously so as not to embarrass the families.

In the spirit of goodwill, we talked about it as a family and decided we would deliver the items ourselves and dress up in Santa hats and give holiday cheer, but tactfully act as *Santa's messengers* so as not to create any embarrassment.

The information we received was that these children were all from needy families who could not afford to provide Christmas gifts for their children.

We arrived at the first home and found no one home, so we waited and eventually moved on, leaving the gifts organized neatly on the front porch with a private note.

The second delivery was in a neighborhood of project housing, and we went to the door expecting to see poverty stricken conditions. We

were instead greeted expectantly by a woman
smoking a clove cigarette, who waived us inside
instructing us to place the gifts on the couch next
to the full service bar and stereo system.

I remember this home distinctly as they had a
television and entertainment system that would
have made me the envy of my neighborhood had
I ever had one. This was not so unsettling, as the
nonchalant attitude of the mother. We were all
left with the sensation that the mother had
written the letters herself and was expecting our
arrival.

Undaunted, we moved on to the next home which
happened to be in the same projects. Once again
we were greeted, waved on inside and told to
place the packages on the couch without so much
as a *'Thank you'* or a *'Merry Christmas'* in return.

The children like the previous houses were
nowhere to be seen. When we inquired about
this, we were told they were out playing in the
neighborhood.

The fourth house greeted us at the door, and took the packages from us without inviting us in or very much conversation, but instead treating us like expected delivery people. At this point our spirits were low, and our inspiration for goodwill was dying.

The final residence was the only one that was a free standing house. We approached the home with trepidation and knocked on the door. We were greeted by a tall and serious looking woman who asked us who we were. When we told her we were Santa's helpers with gifts for the children in response to their Santa letter, she broke her countenance into a smile of jubilation and praise and began looking skyward and thanking Jesus.

She was so genuinely happy and grateful, explaining that she was just laid off from her job prior to the holidays and was struggling to make ends meet. She introduced us to the children, and they were all very happy to receive their presents.

We walked away from that home with a profound sense of well-being. Our inspiration to do further goodwill had been rekindled. We were again rejuvenated from this final experience in the whole adventure.

So I learned that goodwill can become infectious. We continued to do this kind of charity work for the next several Christmases, and although we did run into the ones who were thankless and playing the system, we also helped a few truly needy families and children in the process. We also tried to balance our thoughts on the matter that despite the conduct of their parents, we hoped the children who wrote the letters did experience a happy holiday during those years.

Goodwill can become infectious, but sometimes it takes work to look beyond what one sees before them. It also requires a willingness to look beyond the shortcomings of man, and reach out and help them anyways. For those times when you run into a person who truly is grateful and your gestures rescued them from one of their darkest hours, perhaps that is when the spirit of goodwill becomes the most infectious of all.

Chapter Seven:

An Indelible Love

Having an indelible love in one's life can be quite powerful. I am blessed to have married the most wonderful woman in the world. We have been together over fifteen years now. When we go about our daily lives sometimes with the distractions of work and the demands of living, one can sometimes lose sight, if just for a brief time, how special that is.

One night not long ago, I came home just after midnight from my evening job. My wife had already gone to bed. I drank a cup of green tea alone with our dog in the kitchen before I ventured up to our bedroom to turn in for the night. It had been a long day for me.

Upon entering our bedroom, my wife awoke. She had not been feeling well, and had turned in early. When I entered, she was in serious discomfort with a chest congestion, cough, etc. I sat down with her and gave her a back rub, got her some vitamins and an aspirin for her headache. I also cut up an orange for her from the kitchen, and got her to eat some of it along with some water and vitamin C capsules. I spent the next two hours making sure she could relax, including rubbing and massaging her back which was cramping up with the flu.

As part of her normal morning tasks, she drives our step son to his job in the morning where he has to leave at 6:30am. The next morning I let her sleep, and got up at 6:00am and took him to work instead.

All in all, I perhaps slept 3 hours that night. Do you want to know something? It did not even cross my mind that there was anything usual about this. Having that indelible love in one's life allows you to see beyond the physical demands of the body, the environment, etc. I was alert and although my body was somewhat tired the next day, spiritually I was as bright as or brighter than ever.

When I returned from taking my step-son to work that morning, I brewed some coffee for my wife when she later woke up, and enjoyed some wonderful hours of time with her. She was feeling much better after some rest and the care from the night before.

So from this experience, when I look back on it I can say that there is no greater experience one can ask for in life than to be there for someone you love when they most need it. An indelible love is the most empowering spiritual vitality extant in our universe, and it is to be cherished above all things.

Materialistic concerns are an unsavory, unequal and unsatisfying comparison to the majesty of a spiritual moment or moments with an indelible love. Finding a person you can truly share your life with at that special spiritual level is more valuable and gratifying than all the treasures this world can offer.

Chapter Eight:

The Universal Roar

I once had the opportunity to go to a baseball game that turned out to be one of the greatest experiences of my life. It was October of 1992, and I was living in Atlanta, Georgia.

The Braves baseball team was competing in the National League Championship series, and although they had begun the best of seven series with a 3-1 lead over the Pittsburgh Pirates, they had somehow through errors and lack of hitting lost games 5 and 6. The series was now tied 3-3, and there were many fair-weather fans that were giving up on the Braves winning.

It was the afternoon of the day game seven was to be played, and I encountered a woman who wanted to sell her two tickets for that game for $100 each. She had lost the enthusiasm to go, and decided to watch the game from home. I called Dwight, my brother-in-law, and he said to purchase them *immediately!*

So we were going to the game, and although there was an air of despair cast over the city with the Braves having lost games 5 & 6, we were determined to support our team.

At some point on the drive to the game, I looked at Dwight and said *"You know, we can also just be baseball fans tonight. Someone is going to win the National League Pennant, and either way it is a historical night for baseball."*

So we agreed to just enjoy the spirit of the game, at the very least, so as not to be disappointed if the Braves lost. We parked at a remote parking area with thousands of other fans, and began our long walk to Fulton County Stadium. The night was slightly cool and we were wearing light jackets.

Dwight had brought along a large red wooden tomahawk he had purchased at a roadside stand some weeks before, to display at the in the spirit of the famous Braves fan's 'tomahawk chop'. We attempted to go through the turnstiles with this huge three and a half foot long tomahawk and the security guard told us we could not bring it in, claiming it could be used as a weapon.

I was dismayed, and was not looking forward to walking back to the car to stow it away. I also did not think Dwight wanted to toss it in a dumpster either.

The circular design of Fulton County Stadium proved to be a virtue that night, as there were entrances at multiple points of the circle. After the security guard incident, I was walking through the crowd ahead of Dwight, looking for a trash can or dumpster to dispose of the tomahawk so we could just go in and find our seats. At the same time I was trying to think of ways to convince Dwight to toss it away rather than go back to the car.

I turned around at one point to look for Dwight, and saw that he had a Cheshire grin on his face and was crab walking towards me. He had stashed the tomahawk down the pant leg of his jeans, and had his jacket wrapped around the top of it. He looked at me and said *"Let's go find the next entrance."*

Laughing to myself at the silliness of our venture,
we passed through security without a hitch.
Once inside, Dwight handed the tomahawk to me
and said impishly *"Want a hot dog?"*

I was laughing out loud at this point.

We found our seats, called the vendor over and
secured a few hot dogs and waited for game time.
The game was one for the ages. It also was the
most grueling evenings, as we watched both
teams go scoreless until the 8th inning. At the top
of the 9th inning, the Pirates scored two runs.

The crowd having been optimistic up to that
point was now very worried. I am not exactly
sure if what happened next was the precise
launch of what followed, but it may very well
have been. There was a family of five that were
seated in front of us, and they all got up to leave
when the Pirates scored, leaving a gap in the
continuance of the crowd.

A man in front of me two rows forward turned to
Dwight and myself, and the others around in our

section, and he spoke aloud with conviction. He said *"Look folks, this is it. We either do something together, or the season is over. Let's roar! Let's make noise now, or it is all over!"*

So the people in my row began to pound on the seats in front of us. We began to shout at the top of our lungs. The Braves were coming to bat in the bottom of the 9th, and we were determined to will them to victory! The ripple of seats being drummed began to be repeated from our section and continued throughout the stadium. Soon the entire stadium was shouting at a decibel level unprecedented on the evening so far, with a rhythm of drumming that resembled an army on the warpath.

The stadium had become a universal roar, and things began to happen. A Braves player got a base hit. Then another and we had two men on base, one on third and the other on first after a Pirates error. There were two outs, but we had two men on base!

Then Sid Bream stepped up to the plate. Sid had been the first basemen for the Braves. He was in that position for his adept skill, but not for his ability to run. He had bad knees, and was a typical slow mover around the bases. However, Sid was the man at bat and he could hit. We all began to drum our seats, and I grabbed the tomahawk and began to swing it and pound it against the seat.

That night, it could be said that Bream hit the single heard around the world. He sent that ball into center field, a solid single, and proceeded to round the bases. We had scored a run and another. Everyone assumed incorrectly that Sid would be stopped at third by the coach, with the score now tied, but instead *he was waved home!*

He ran with all his might and the crowd roared even louder than before and Sid Bream crossed that plate as the ball sailed in from the outfield. When the ball reached the catcher and Bream crossed the plate almost in unison, there was a moment of deadly silence until umpire gave the sign for *'Safe!'* and the stadium erupted like never before. *The Brave's had miraculously won!*

I have never hugged so many strangers in my life. I saw Dwight being bear hugged by men twice his size, and lifting him up in joyous celebration. Women were kissing strangers, and people were dancing in their seats. No one wanted to leave the stadium for hours, as we watched the trophy ceremony and the newscasts and replays on the big screen over and over.

The braves had won in the bottom of the ninth, in a walk off victory and it was a moment like no other in history for the town. I remember little about the exiting of the stadium or the walk to the car, but I do remember the honking of horns for hours as the caravan of cars found their way out onto the highways.

The next day the newspaper carried a minor story buried under the greater story of the victory. That small story was that they had discovered over 300 seats in Fulton County Stadium were damaged or broken after the game, and would need to be replaced. I smiled a knowing smile to myself, having experienced the real story, because I had been there. I did not break a seat that night, but I know I wanted to.

To my knowledge no one in my section did either, but I am sure others following our lead likely got carried away in the moment.

To this day the memory of that evening in Atlanta at game 7 of the NLCS was something I will never forget. It was a great moment in baseball, but more importantly it was the experience of being part of a universal roar. To be so connected for a short time with so many thousands of people passionately crying out for a unified purpose for our beloved team and willing them to victory.

It is a connection with ones fellow man that seldom happens, and not everyone gets to experience such a moment. There are few words that can describe the sensation of thousands of voices and the rhythm of thunder vibrating through ones entire body at the height of spiritual ecstasy. It was enough to inspire perfection in those last few moments of the game in the players that felt it. It was enough to make the impossible possible.

Imagine, if you will, taking such an event to a higher level: consider the idea of having all the people of earth unified in one resounding roar together inspiring us all on to our own greatest moment. Imagine the feeling and the sensation, and the vibration of all the souls of earth willing us all on to greatness. If you imagine it long and hard enough, you might also feel a special touch and connection with your fellow man, and life may never be the same for you again.

Chapter Nine:

The Human Touch

There was a time about a year prior to this writing where my wife went to stay with her mother in Bogota, Colombia for a period of about 5 months over the winter. Her mother had been ill, and she needed some care and attention to help put some order in her life. Also, my wife had just retired from a job she had for over 20 years, and was looking for a little respite from the Michigan weather.

I stayed home to work through the winter months, and took care of the homestead. During this time I went to work daily, and worked on my writing projects in the evenings and weekends.

Through the magic of the inter-connected world we live in, I would stay in touch with my wife daily via Skype and or Facetime on our iPhones. Although we never were wholly without communication with each other, I found after the second or third month that I longed to have her closer. There was a profound absence in my life.

One evening a new awareness struck me. My schedule and my jobs were very much independent jobs without much human contact directly with people. I would see the receptionists at my night job when I arrived, and then would proceed to my office alone to work for the evening answering calls from prospective clients, etc.

My day job as a Realtor put me more in contact with people, however, in the months of December through February, I found myself avoiding the task of going out to show houses due to the cold temperatures. In effect, I was purposely not interacting with many people in this job as I have gotten older the winter weather has been less friendly for me. So having the opportunity to scale down my business in this area to a lighter schedule, I did so.

Perhaps it was the winter, and the cold, or perhaps it was the change of my schedule and my life routine. I realized that after a time, I longed for the human touch. Although I had been around people, I had not touched anyone physically in months. The discovery was quite peculiar.

I became aware of the necessity of human contact. Be it a hand shake or a hand on the shoulder or a hug now and then. Connecting with another person is a good thing. It is the media and television in America that has created a society where people are afraid to touch each other. Through fear they have successfully created the mythical generality that touching is *'inappropriate physical contact'*. Therefore driven by fear of offending someone or being accused or charged with this *inappropriate physical conduct*, people hearing this message over and over again tend to withdraw from touching each other.

There is nothing wrong with a hug. There is nothing wrong with a hearty handshake, a kiss on the cheek or a hand on the shoulder. This fear of touching each other is a media created cultural fear driven propaganda campaign.

Is there inappropriate touching? Of course there
is. There has been and always will be the
occasional creep who gropes and pokes or
touches someone inappropriately. This does not
mean that everyone does this. In fact those that
do are in the minority, and if they do it in front of
others usually will get a black eye from someone
justifiably and well deserved. The civilized 99%
of us do not have to live in fear that we will be
likened to that uncouth and boorish remaining
1%.

I think we all know what is inappropriate
conduct, and also what is civilized conduct, and
we do not need an agenda driven media or
government agency to tell us, much less regulate
us on the matter. Having realized that I had not
been in physical contact with another person for
several months, I decided to test my theory.

When I went to work that evening, instead of
walking past the receptionist, I placed my hand
on the young ladies shoulder and said *"I have
never thanked you for doing such a great job.
Thank you!"* Did she scream or withdraw from
this human touch? No, she smiled and sincerely

said *"Thank you"* in return and there was a connection of affinity between us. She felt uplifted because someone noticed her, and I felt good to be able to give her the compliment she so well deserved. In addition, the hand on the shoulder was a meaningful gesture of kindness. I was also put back in contact briefly with the human race.

The next day, I went to a meeting the Board of Realtors and walked up to a colleague of mine and said *"Bill! I have not seen you in awhile, give me a hug!"* You know what he did? He smiled and hugged me, and I bear hugged him back. Once again I felt the warmth of sincere friendship. Do you know what happened next? Someone else walked up and said they wanted to hug Bill too, and did so. My forward gesture of friendship inspired others to do the same.

At the grocery store a few days later, I observed am elderly woman having a hard time finding something on a shelf. I walked over to her and placed my hand on her shoulder and inquired *"Ma'am, can I help you find something?"* She immediately responded with *"I am trying to find*

canned olives and left my damn glasses in the car!"
I laughed, and helped her find the olives which
were on a shelf one row over. She thanked me
warmly, and reached out and placed both of her
hands on mine and said *"You are a kind man"*.

The human touch with another is important. I
believe we are all connected. I would venture to
guess that if you sent a man alone into outer
space and left him alone for months, you would
find he would go a bit crazy. In fact the Russians
sent Cosmonauts on such missions alone, and
reportedly came back a little loony.

If one travels to certain countries in Europe, such
as Italy or Greece, the human touch is a vibrant
part of their culture. Greetings are not a mere
waving of the hand, but a hug and a kiss on the
cheek. They would laugh someone right out of
the country if they tried to forward a campaign of
no touching as has been created on America.

One time in the early 1990's after the Berlin wall
had come down that separated East and West
Germany, I traveled with my brother-in-law,
Dwight, to Germany to visit a small village that

was populated with glass makers, so that we could establish business relations. We had rented a car at the Frankfurt airport, and drove over to the former East Germany side of the country to find this village and find a bed and breakfast to stay at.

When we crossed over to what used to be East Germany, the road signage became scarce and the houses started to be less colorful, having been covered by gray of soot from the forty years of burning coal as a fuel. The Eastern Germans were forty years behind in their municipal infrastructure, and since the reunification they were for the first time, getting natural gas lines installed. However, the process was going to take several more years, so many villages we passed through were still burning coal as fuel at that time to get through winter.

Within about a half hour of crossing over into former East Germany, we were lost. It was snowing and sleeting, and it was approaching 11:00pm. We needed to stop to get our bearings. Dwight pulled the car into the only business that had its lights on, which was a liquor store.

I stayed in the car and tried to decipher the map. Dwight went in search of someone to ask directions, hoping to find someone that understood English as our Deutsch was quite poor. As he left the driver's side of the car, he passed in front of the vehicle and I watched him in the car headlights through the windshield approach this large German man who was coming out of the store.

I could see them converse with each other, but the windows were rolled up and it was sleeting, so I watched the conversation take place out of hearing distance through the movement of the wiper blades. After a few minutes of watching Dwight speaking to this man with animated gestures, I witnessed something remarkable. The man put down the bag he was carrying, and wrapped both his arms around Dwight and lifted him off the ground a few inches in a tremendous hug. He was smiling, and animated and pointed down the road and was obviously giving him directions.

When Dwight returned to the car, he was smiling and laughing. He told me that the man as soon as he found out he was an American proclaimed that he wanted to hug him because he had never met an American until now in his own country. He told him that he had longed to see the Americans for many years come through the wall and rescue his country from the East German communism. He was more than happy to help, and gave us directions which enabled us to find the village we were searching for.

This incident stuck with me for many years. I have come to realize that this man like so many of us had a longing for the human touch of friendship. The East Germans had longed for contact for forty years with the West, and they dreamed of getting over the wall and finding a way to America, England or anywhere else in Europe than where they were. The entire body of a nation longed for that human touch of friendship across borders.

So if you have ever had the doubt of the importance of touching someone, even a stranger, do not fear this desire to do so. Do not let others strike fear in your heart to touch another person. Become aware that anyone who forwards that message is trying to forward an insidious campaign of misery.

Even as I write this, my dog has jumped on my shoulder reminding me that I have not petted him in an hour and is demanding physical contact. Our furry friends are well acquainted with this basic spiritual necessity in life. It is what connects us all, and brings us together. Go out and hug a friend, loved one, a pet or even a stranger today. It may seem like an intangible, but you will feel happier if you do.

Chapter Ten:

Discovery & Enlightenment

The greatest notion that anyone could get into their heads is the notion that they never stop learning. To put it bluntly, it is a sad story to consider that so many people think the need for discovering the world around them stops when they graduate high school or college.

The truth of the matter is that there is always more to learn. Life is a continual journey of discovery and enlightenment. One can never adopt the idea that there is not more to know or learn. When you do that, your world gets that much smaller.

Here are five tips to apply in your life to keep your own wheels of discovery rolling even in this internet age of speed and connectivity:

Read a new book or eBook at least once a month, preferably once a week. Choose a subject you have interest in. Trying to read a book or continue to read a book you have no interest in will only dampen your spirits and stop you from reading and learning.

Try something new you have never tried before. Do this at least every month or every week. This could mean going to a place you never have gone to before in your community, or just looking up a new activity you can engage yourself in online.

Draw up a list of improvements you would like to see in your environment. This could be painting your bedroom, organizing your bookshelves, or closet. Whatever the project, write it down and take on the challenge to complete one of these items a month minimally.

Go out in the world once a week and introduce yourself to someone you have never met before. Go sit on a park bench next to someone and ask them to share some stories with you about their life. See what you can discover, and it will amaze you.

Go throughout your day or week, and look for things you do not understand. Seek to find the meaning, origin or source of the misunderstanding and learn what you can about it. It could be a word, a phrase or a symbol. It could even be an unknown object. Do these as frequently as you can and consult a dictionary, encyclopedia or research online. Soon you will find you are learning new things daily or weekly.

There should never be an end to discovery and enlightenment in one's life. These bring about an expansion of awareness and clarity of thought and understanding. Distance yourself from people and ideas that would encourage you to do otherwise.

The journey through life is traveled on the road of curiosity which leads to the halls of wisdom. Don't ever venture far from the path of constant learning. If you follow the five tips above, you will always be finding new things to learn and you will feel a spiritual expansion continually in your life.

Chapter Eleven:

The Heart of the Matter

It has long been stated that at the root of compassion lies the Golden Rule: *"Do unto others as you would have them do unto you."* It also has been written: *"Do not treat other as you would not like them to treat you."* There are several other variations on this concept with the centralized theme of stepping outside of oneself and caring for another above all self-interest.

We live in a world today that has distanced itself from compassion, and quite often allows a spiritually detached media to submit to the population a doctrine of fear and intolerance on a global scale. It is often fed to those who listen in the form of a diet of shock and scandal, blanketed by an ideology of universal hopelessness designed to bring about apathy and despair.

In effect the way the world news is selected and handed to us as the message of 'what is happening globally' is akin to the absurdity of a vintner choosing only the handful of rotten fruit from a scattering of isolated plants and proclaiming this is the condition of the entire vineyard.

Compassion and understanding get lost in this mix of noise and misdirection. It is no wonder the average human being is suspicious of someone who reaches out to help them.

Just the other day I was in a grocery store and came across a little boy of perhaps 7 or 8 years of age crying for his mother. He did not know where she was, and was distraught. Other adults were walking right past him, ignoring him. I abandoned my grocery cart and walked over to him and asked him: *"did you lose your mommy?"*

He tearfully opened his eyes and looked up to me and said *"Yes..."*

I looked at him and said "How about I help you find her?"

He cried and said *"Okay..."*

So I walked him through the store until we found his mother. She was grateful for the help, and scolded him for wandering off.

I thought to myself after that incident, *why didn't anyone else step forward?* Then I realized that someone did. *I had stepped up to help.*

I began to think about my own childhood, and recalled a time when my brother and I were with our family staying at a campground. We had gone off to play deep into the woods, and gotten seriously lost. We came upon two men in our wanderings through the woods who helped us find our way back. They were camping in the woods, and walked with us several miles until we were safely back with our parents. As soon as they had gotten us to our campground, they disappeared into the woods back to their campsite and I never saw them again.

Upon remembering that incident, I began to think that perhaps it was my turn to help another child like I had been helped. That was why I was placed in that circumstance. It was not because I was more alert than the other adults walking around I realized, it was because in a sense of Karma, it was my time to return the favor.

So compassion and understanding come from the heart. They are within us, and there is perhaps a universal circle where when good is done to us that we must in turn do the same for others. When that circle is broken by the purveyors of bad news and divisionism of the populace through false ideas and archaic concepts such as racism, religious bigotry and sexism, it is easy to lose sight of the necessity for compassion and kindness.

The heart of the matter would be thus: *When you are compassionate and caring for another, and bestow upon them kindness, the goodwill from such a gesture flows like a comforting river through our society and the result can be a peaceful global community working together.*

What goes around does indeed come back around, so make sure what you send around is good. If you can truly understand this, you will realize that you are in control of compassion. It is within you, and you can originate kindness to others without having to have a reason to do so. You do not have to wait to be reminded of a time another helped you before you can act.

Therefore, if you go about without motivation with a mindset that you will sincerely help others, and be considerate of those around you, it can only result in your own serenity and well-being. Call it a self-generated inspiration for compassion, or a random act of kindness. Whatever the description, it is a broader scale practice of the Golden Rule that we would all be better off if all of us could live by it.

72

Chapter Twelve:

A Walk on the Lighter Side...

What if you could take a walk through a park in a public place, like Central Park in New York and just make people happy? Have you ever considered just taking a few hours out of your day to make this your quest?

You might ask *"Why would I do this?"* Sure, you have other things to do. You probably have many more important things to attend to, for certain. However, if you do take on this challenge, consider the following:

What if you walked up to a stranger and paid them a compliment making them smile, or feel good about themselves. What if they in turn felt inspired to do the same with another? And what if that person did the same? Could we not conclude the possibility that making a stranger feel better might result in a ripple effect? You will not know unless you try.

One can never assume one knows what the
outcome will be, or whether or not it will work.
That is the beauty of this kind of creation.

I once met a man who worked behind a counter
at a coffee house in New York City. He had been
serving a multitude of customers, and was not
smiling. I approached the counter when it was
my turn, and placed my order. Before he could
turn away, I said to him *"I also wanted to
compliment you on your skill and talent. You did
an amazing job keeping the line moving and the
customers happy."* He looked at me and smiled
and said *"It was no problem, really"*.

I dined in at a table within view of the counter,
and noticed that after my conversation with him
he was much more cheerful and was much
friendlier with the customers he was serving.
The impact of a kind word to him, perhaps at a
time when he was feeling frustrated or
overwhelmed cheered him up, and he passed
along that good feeling to his other customers.

Now, what if you took it a step further? What if
you sat down at a writing desk and took some

nice stationary and envelopes and wrote out an inspiring note to someone you have not met yet. You could say something such as:

"You are an amazing individual. No matter what hardships or challenges you have experienced, know that you have an infinite potential in you to do great things. You deserve to give yourself another chance the next time you have a setback in life, simply because of the wonderful and unique individual you are. There is no one like you."

Leave the note unsigned. Write nine more of similar complimenting fashion and style. Place each inside an envelope, and go for a walk in Central Park and look for ten people who look as if they need some words of encouragement. Walk up to them; say *"I wrote this for you. I thought you could use it."* Hand them the note, and walk away.

Go hide behind a tree and watch them read it. You will perhaps witness something you only ever dreamed of. The experience of lifting another stranger's burden by the simple use of kind words of encouragement.

I like to call this *'A walk on the lighter side'.* It is a walk I encourage you to take. Pass along some words of encouragement, and kindness. If you do this, others might also follow your lead and do it themselves. Together we could start a new movement of helping and encouraging each other, and bringing the world together that much closer.

Final Thoughts

Living the magic of life takes some commitment, and a desire for continued spiritual discovery. It requires that one step out of one's own universe for a time, and influence the universe of others.

It also requires a degree of courage to communicate. It requires developing the skill to imbue another with kindness and compassion.

Before courage, however, there is the requirement of willingness to look. It requires a personal decision to consider one's own connection with their fellow man, and the world of humanity. It also must be driven with the passion and confidence that one can make a change in this world, and that one is a significant player in life's events.

To embrace these things, and begin *living the magic* finally requires that one not live one's life in a materialistic solidity, but instead learn to *walk on the lighter side.*

Be willing to laugh, hug, celebrate and cheer for yourself and your fellow man. Embrace our differences and our idiosyncrasies, and the unearthliness of our unified spiritual connection.

In doing so, arm in arm, we will *walk on the lighter side* together.

ABOUT THE AUTHOR

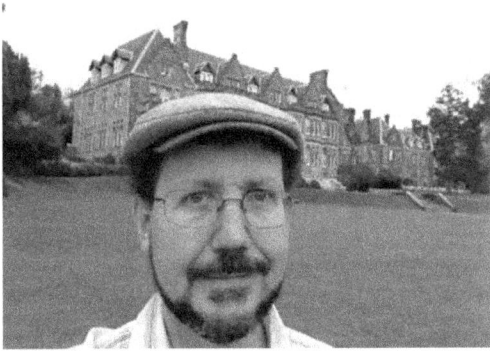

Michael Delaware is a Phoenix, Arizona native who now resides in Battle Creek, Michigan with his wife Margarita. He also lived in Georgia for 15 years in the 1980's and 1990's where he owned and operated a stained and beveled glass studio in the Metro-Atlanta area. He has been a Michigan resident since 1999.

His other published works include numerous non-fiction books on real estate, sales management, marketing and other self-help topics. He has also published fiction and non-fiction stories for children.

As an illustrator and photographer, he has included his works in his own books and blogs.

He enjoys hiking and mountain biking in the great outdoors and taking long walks in the woods with his dog.

Currently he is an active Realtor in Michigan and frequent community volunteer. He is a member of the National Association of Realtors, The Council of Residential Specialists, and the Michigan Association of Realtors. He is also an active member of the Battle Creek Area Association of Realtors where he was awarded 'Realtor of the Year' in 2010, and served as Board President in 2011. He founded his own independent publishing company in 2012.

To follow Michael:

**www.MichaelDelaware.com
Facebook.com/MichaelDelawareAuthor
Amazon.com/Author/MichaelDelaware
Linkedin.com/in/MichaelDelaware
@MichaelDelaware**

Other titles by the author:

(Available in paperback and eBook format unless otherwise noted)

The Art of Sales Management: Lessons Learned on the Fly

The Art of Sales Management: Revelations of a Goal Maker

The Art of Sales Management: 75 Training Drills to Build Confidence, Excellence & Teamwork

Small Business Sales Management: 19 Winning Secrets of Success

Small Business Marketing: An Insider's Collection of Secrets

Arts & Craft Shows: The Top 10 Mistakes Artist Vendors Make... *And How to Avoid Them!*

Arts & Craft Shows: 12 Secrets Every Artist Vendor Should Know

Inspiration: The Journey of a Lifetime *(eBook only)*

For Real Estate:

Understanding Land Contract Homes: In Pursuit of the American Dream

Land Contract Homes for Investors

Land Contract Homes: The Top 10 Mistakes Home Buyers Make... *And How to Avoid Them!*

Going Home... Renting to Home Ownership in 10 Easy Steps

In Children's Fiction:

Scary Elephant Meets the Closet Monster *(eBook only)*

In Children's Non-Fiction:

My Name is Blue: The Story of a Rescue Dog *(eBook only)*

For a current list of available print books visit:
Amazon.com/Author/MichaelDelaware